Music Lesson 2

What Makes Sound?

SonLight Education Ministry
United States of America

Copyright © 1996 by
SonLight Education Ministry
www.sonlighteducation.com

*You may use these materials for your immediate family,
classroom, or study group. No portion of this material
may be reproduced for profit, sold, or used for financial benefit.
This material belongs to SonLight Education Ministry
and is not to be distributed as the property
of any other person, ministry, or organization.*

A Suggested Daily Schedule

(Adapt this schedule to your family needs.)

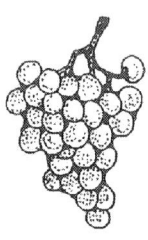

5:00 a.m.	Arise–Personal Worship
6:00 a.m.	Family Worship and Bible Class–With Father
7:00 a.m.	Breakfast
8:00 a.m.	Practical Arts*–Domestic Activities Agriculture Industrial Arts (especially those related to the School Lessons)
10:00 a.m.	School Lessons (Take a break for some physical exercise during this time slot.)
12:00 p.m.	Dinner Preparations (Health class could be included at this time or a continued story.)
1:00 p.m.	Dinner
2:00 p.m.	Practical Arts* or Fine Arts (Music and Crafts) (especially those related to the School Lessons)
5:00 p.m.	Supper
6:00 p.m.	Family Worship–Father (Could do History Class)
7:00 p.m.	Personal time with God–Bed Preparation
8:00 p.m.	Bed

*Daily nature walk can be in morning or afternoon.

The Desire of All Nations

This book is a part of a curriculum that is built upon the life of Christ entitled, "The Desire of All Nations," for grades 2-8. Any of the books in this curriculum can be used by themselves or as an entire program.

INFORMATION ABOUT THE 2-8 GRADE PROGRAM

Multi-level

This program is written on a multi-level. That means that each booklet has material for grades 2-8. This is so the whole family in these grades may work from the same books. It is difficult for a busy mother to have 2 or more children and each have a different set of books. Remember, the Bible is written for all ages.

The Bible—the Primary Textbook

The books in this program are designed to teach the parent and the student how to learn academic subjects by using the Bible as a primary textbook.

The Desire of Ages

The Desire of Ages by Ellen G. White is used as a textbook to go with the Bible. This focuses on the early life of Christ, when He was a child. Children relate best to Christ as a child and youth.

Lesson Numbers

The big number in the top right corner on the cover of this book is the Lesson Number and corresponds with the chapter number in the book *The Desire of Ages*. For example, Lesson 1 in the school program will go along with chapter 1 in *The Desire of Ages*. Usually each family starts at the beginning with Lesson 1. Most children have not had a true Bible program, therefore they need the foundation built. If there is academic material that they have already covered, they do the Bible part and review then pass quickly on.

Seven Academic Subjects

There are seven academic subjects in this program—Health, Mathematics, Music, Science–Nature, History/Geography/Prophecy, Language, Voice–Speech.

Language Program

A good, solid language program is recommended to be used along with the SonLight materials.

The Riggs Institute has a multi-sensory teaching method that accommodates every child's unique learning style. Their program is called *Writing and Spelling Road to Reading and Thinking*. Order by calling (800) 200-4840 or visit www.riggsinst.org. (Disclaimer: SonLight does not endorse the reading books recommended in the Riggs' program.)

Another option which you might find more user friendly and is similar to the Riggs program but from a Christian perspective is *Spell to Write and Read* by Wanda Sanseri. To order, call Wanda Sanseri at (503) 654-2300 or visit https://www.bhibooks.net/swr.html

"God's Chosen People"
Lesson 2 – Diligence

The following books are those you will need for this lesson.
All of these can be obtained from www.sonlighteducation.com

The Rainbow Covenant – Study the spiritual meaning of colors and make your own rainbow book.

Health
The Body

Math
A Place

Music
What Makes Sound?

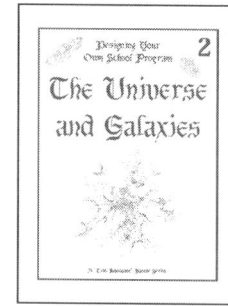

Science/Nature
The Universe and Galaxies

A Casket – Coloring book and story. Learn how to treat the gems of the Bible.

H/G/P
The Earth

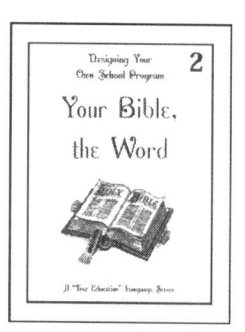

Language
Your Bible, the Word

Speech/Voice
Care of the Voice

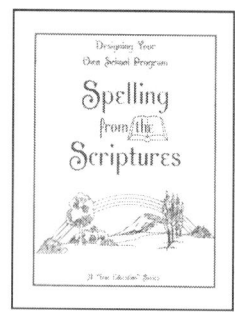

Spelling from the Scriptures

Bible Study – Learn how to study the Bible and helpful use tools.

Bible
The Desire of all Nations I
Teacher Study Guide

Student Study Guide

Bible Lesson Study Guide

Memory Verses
The Desire of all Nations I
Scripture Songs Book
and MP3 files

Our Nature Study Book – Your personal nature journal.

iv

Table of Contents

Teacher Section	Pages 1-8
Student Section	Pages 1-30

Research
A Certain Sound	Page 1
Reinforce	Page 3
Remind	Page 3
Reflect – Distinct Sounds	Page 4
Reinforce – A Distinct Sound	Page 5
Learning How to Be **Diligent**	Page 6
Reinforce	Page 7
What Does it Mean to **Diligently** Give a Certain Sound?	Page 8
Reflect	Page 8
Diligence – Statements and Answers	Page 9
"More **Diligence**" – Song	Page 9
Reflect	Page 9
Reinforce	Page 10
Distinct Sounds through the Centuries	Page 11
Remind	Page 12
Reinforce	Page 12
Reflect – A Certain Sound through the Centuries	Page 13
Sympathetic Vibration	Page 14
Reflect	Page 14
Reflect – Vibrations	Page 15
Remind	Page 16
Reinforce	Page 16

Research
How Wind Instruments Make Sound	Page 17
Reinforce	Page 17
"Stand Up, Stand Up For Jesus" – Story	Page 18
"Stand Up, Stand Up For Jesus" – Poem	Page 19

Table of Contents

Two Types of Wind Instruments
    (1) Woodwinds — Page 20
    Remarkable Fact — Page 20
        "Woodwind Instruments" – Illustration — Page 21
  (2) Brass — Page 22
    Reinforce – A Certain Sound — Page 22
        "Brass Instruments" – Illustration — Page 23
        "Little Performances" – Story — Page 24
    Review — Page 25
    Reinforce — Page 26
Remainder – An Uncertain Sound — Page 27
    Reflect — Page 27
        "Sounds" – Mark Your Bible — Page 28
        "Wind Instruments" – Mark Your Bible — Page 30

Teacher Section

"Blessed is the people
that know the joyful sound:
they shall walk, O Lord,
in the light of thy countenance."
Psalm 89:15

INSTRUCTIONS For the Teacher

Step 1

Study the Bible Lesson and begin to memorize the Memory Verses. Familiarize Yourself With the Character Quality. The student can answer the Bible Review Questions. See page 6. Use the Steps in Bible Study.

Bible Lesson

God's Chosen People – Exodus 20:3-6; Psalm 115:4-8; Isaiah 43:10, 11; 49:3-6; 56:7; Ezra 9:5-7; Romans 1:22-23

Memory Verses

Isaiah 56:7; Deuteronomy 26:18-19; 28:10; 4:5-6

Character Quality

Diligence – constant effort to accomplish what is undertaken; exertion of body or mind without unnecessary delay or sloth; due attention; industry

Antonyms – dilatoriness; slowness; casualness; slothfulness

Character Quality Verses

Colossians 3:23 – *"And whatsoever ye do, do it heartily, as to the Lord, and not unto men."*

Proverbs 4:23 – *"Keep thy heart with all **diligence**; for out of it are the issues of life."*

Step 2

Understand How To/And

A. Do the Spelling Cards so the student can begin to build his own spiritual dictionary.

B. Mark Your Bible.

C. Evaluate Your Student's Character in relation to the character quality of **diligence**.

D. Familiarize Yourself with *What Makes Sound*, and how it works. Notice the Projects.

E. Review the Scripture References for *What Makes Sound*.

F. Notice the Answer Key.

A. Spelling Cards

Spelling Lists

Music Words
Place I - II - III
brass
certain
column
distinct
noise
pleasant
sound
travel
vibrate
vibration
waves
wind
woodwinds

Place II - III
centuries
instrument
sympathetic

Bible Words
chosen
covenant
diligent
fools
glorified
graven
idols
image
iniquities
jealous
light
likeness
professing
restore
servant
serve
trespass
witnesses
wise

(Teacher, you could add the names of the wind instruments to this list.)

> See the booklet *Spelling from the Scriptures* for instructions about how to make the Spelling Cards.

B. How to Mark the Bible

1. Copy the list of Bible texts in the back of the Bible on an empty page as a guide.

2. Go to the first text in the Bible and copy the next text beside it. Go to the next one and repeat the process until they are all chain-referenced.

3. Have the student present the study to family and/or friends.

4. In each student lesson there are one or more sections that have a Bible marking study on the subject studied. (See the Student's Section, page 28.)

C. Evaluate Your Student's Character

This section is for the purpose of helping the teacher know how to encourage the students in becoming more **diligent**. See page 7.

> Place I = Grades 2-3-4
> Place II = Grades 4-5-6
> Place III = Grades 6-7-8

What Makes Sound? – Teacher – Page 2

D. Familiarize Yourself with What Makes Sound? – Notice the Projects

Projects

1. Teach your child, when asked to do a chore, to answer with a pleasant, polite voice, "Yes, mother" or "Yes, father." Remember the sound of your voice is to make known the character of God. Speak distinctly.

2. As you are working together as a family, **diligently** practice having a musical sound to your voice when visiting or speaking to one another in the family.

3. Think of creative ways to **diligently** sound the message that Christ is coming soon. Keep some tracts in your car to give away as you have opportunity.

4. Have the student read I Corinthians 14:7-8 and Romans 10:18. Have the student explain what these verses are saying. Discuss as a family. Look up the word "sound" in the *Strong's Concordance* from the above two verses. What does it mean? How do these verses relate to the Bible story, "The Chosen People."

5. Using your Nature Study Book list all the things you hear in nature that make sound.

7. Make a study notebook on either ants or beavers.

A. Find pictures.
B. Find information.
C. Put it together in an organized fashion.

8. If no one in your family plays a wind instrument, find someone who will play and show you how it works.

E. Review the Scripture References for *What Makes Sound*

Teacher, read through this section before working on the lesson with the student. See page 28 in the Student Section.

F. Notice the Answer Key

The Answer Key for the student book is found on page 8.

Step 3

Read the Lesson Aim.

Lesson Aim

The purpose of this lesson is to gain a deeper understanding of what the laws of music are by exploring sound and what makes sound. The student will also learn how this relates to God's chosen people. God created music to serve a purpose just as His chosen people are to serve a purpose. This lesson will help the student to understand what that purpose is, and how, through **diligent** practice and study, they can help fulfill that purpose through music.

God's purpose for Israel was that they would **diligently** sound God's character to the world, that the world might know Him and be prepared for Christ's first coming. Instead, they fixed their hopes on worldly greatness, and just as musical sound waves get weaker and weaker the farther they travel from the source of vibration, God's people became weaker and weaker as they moved away from God and turned to their own ways. Their sound then came from another source which misrepresented God's character. They became a noise. God still wants His people to **diligently** sound the message that Christ is coming again soon and to make His character known by the music of their lives. *"For from you <u>sounded out</u> the word of the Lord...in every place your faith to God-ward is spread abroad"* (I Thessalonians 1:8).

Step 4

Prepare to begin the Music Lesson.

To Begin the Music Lesson

Make a list of all the sounds that you hear on a regular basis in your home. Discuss what causes them. Are they man-made sounds or sounds God created in the beginning?

What is your favorite musical instrument that you enjoy hearing or playing?

Step 5

These lessons are designed for the whole family. Begin the Music Lesson. Cover only what can be understood by your student. Make the lessons a family project by all being involved in part or all of them.

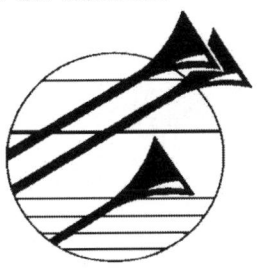

Steps in Bible Study

1. Prayer

2. Read the verses/meditate/memorize.

3. Look up key words in *Strong's Concordance* and find their meaning in the Hebrew or Greek dictionary in the back of that book.

4. Cross reference (marginal reference) with other Bible texts. An excellent study tool is *The Treasury of Scripture Knowledge*.

5. Use Bible custom books for more information on the times.

6. Write a summary of what you have learned from those verses.

7. Mark key thoughts in the margin of your Bible.

8. Share your study with others to reinforce the lessons you have learned.

Review Questions

1. What religious worship prevailed anciently? (Romans 1:22, 23; Psalm 115:4-8)

2. What was the great mission of the chosen people, Israel? (Exodus 20:3-6; Isaiah 43:10, 11; 49:3-6; 56:7)

3. How did they fail in their duty? (Ezra 9:5-7)

4. Thought Question: How did God overrule Israel's failure in not accomplishing His purpose or their mission?

5. What three nations or races were most influential in the civilized world at the time of Christ? For what was each remarkable? (a. Rome–Law; b. Greeks–Language; c. Jews–Religion)

6. What had each contributed to prepare the way for the spread of the gospel? (a. Rome – Government; b. Greek – Language; c. Jews – Knowledge of the true God)

7. God prepared the Gentile world for the coming of the Redeemer by:
a. System of heathenism had lost its hold on the people
b. Bible had been translated into Greek and was the universal language
c. Some Jews remained steadfast and true to the true God
d. Palestine was the center of the world's gatherings

8. Who are God's chosen people today? (His faithful followers)

Questions 5, 6 and 7 will need to be asked and then answered by the teacher.

Evaluating Your Child's Character

Check the appropriate box for your student's level of development, or your own, as the case may be.

Maturing Nicely (MN), Needs Improvement (NI), Poorly Developed (PD), Absent (A)

Diligence

1. Does the student have difficulty in following through on assigned tasks without being reminded?

   Yes ☐   No ☐

2. Does the student tend to take on the responsibilities of others, leaving his/her own responsibilities unattended?

   Yes ☐   No ☐

3. Is the student able to complete tasks in spite of distractions?

   Yes ☐   No ☐

4. Does the student need constant supervision in order to perform at their best level?

   Yes ☐   No ☐

5. Is the time that a child can wait between achievement and reward increasing appreciably?

   MN ☐   NI ☐   PD ☐   A ☐

6. Does the student move quickly and efficiently on the job, or does he move slowly?

   MN ☐   NI ☐   PD ☐   A ☐

7. Does the student look forward to the job or complains about the task?

   MN ☐   NI ☐   PD ☐   A ☐

8. Does the student first do the job to please the Lord and then his parents?

   MN ☐   NI ☐   PD ☐   A ☐

What Makes Sound? – Teacher – Page 7

Answer Key

Page 10

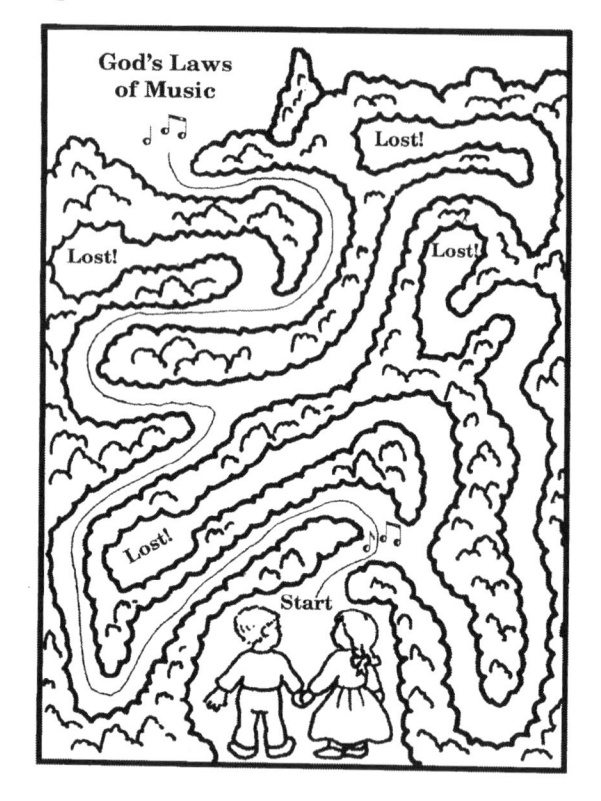

Page 25

1. "To make known"

2. See page 1.

3. No

4. See pages 6-9.

5. "To swing or move back and forth"

6. See pages 1-3.

7. Clear, easily heard, or understood, plain

Page 25 continued

8. Noise can be destructive and pure musical sounds uplifting.

9. Song, prophecy, temple rite, household prayer

10. They were to preserve among men the knowledge of God's law, and the knowledge of the coming Redeemer. They were to reveal God to men by their lives. They expected a king and not a humble baby.

11. If two strings of an instrument are stretched out side by side and tuned to the same pitch, when one is sounded, the other will also sound.

12. (A) higher, (B) lower, (C) higher, (D) lower, (E) lower, (F) higher

13. Teacher, check. Some possible answers are: Moses, at the burning bush, Saul on the road to Damascus, etc.

14. Student, answer.

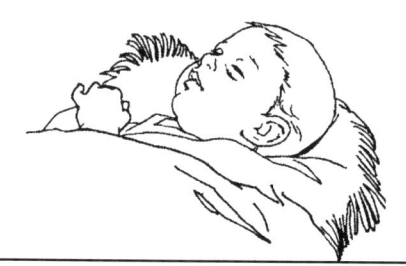

What Makes Sound? – Teacher – Page 8

Gardening Sheet

Lesson Two   Music

Title "What Makes Sound?"

In Season

(This is for In Season and Out of Season.)

A most pleasant <u>sound</u> is a family enjoying the fruits of their diligent labor as they eat their meals of garden vegetables and fruits. It is <u>music</u> to the ear.

Making a plan before you pick up your hoe will give a well ordered garden.

Plan succession plantings so you will not have a feast followed by famine. It helps to garden on paper first.

Feast

Famine

Out of Season

As in good music there is beautiful <u>sound</u> and harmony so in successful gardening there will be pleasant experiences.

However, it is best to always plan ahead—draw a plan!

Play beautiful music while drawing your garden sketch.

Student Section

"And all the congregation worshipped, and the singers sang, and the trumpeters sounded...."
II Chronicles 29:28

What Makes Sound?

Research

A Certain Sound

"And even things without life giving sound, whether pipe or harp, except they give a distinction in the sounds, how shall it be known what is piped or harped? "For if the trumpet give an uncertain sound, who shall prepare himself to the battle?"
I Corinthians 14:7-8

"Hearken unto me"

Stop, go outside, and be quiet for a moment. Listen. What do you hear? Do you hear the chirping of a cricket, trees swaying in the breeze, birds caroling forth their happy songs, or an owl hooting? These may be sounds you hear everyday. Sounds are all around us. When someone plays a trumpet, a harp, the keys on a piano, drinks from a glass, or pets the cat, sound is produced. All of these are common sounds—yet, each are different from the other. The word sound means "to make known." When a dog barks he makes himself known.

Israel was to make known to the world that Jesus was coming. They were not **diligent** in their understanding of the Scriptures. Thus, they were unable to give a certain sound announcing Christ's coming. Today, we are to make known Jesus' second coming to the world. Are we being **diligent** in our understanding of these events? Or are we like those mentioned in Luke 7:32, *"...We have piped unto you, and ye have not danced; we have mourned to you, and ye have not wept."*

Without air there would be no sound. That means that above the atmosphere around the earth there is no sound. If you went into space, above the air around this planet, it would be silent.

When a gun is fired on the top of a high mountain the sound is no louder than a firecracker. But deep in the mines it is just the reverse. So dense is the air that the workmen must talk in whispers, otherwise their voices would be unpleasantly loud. In the arctic regions the air is so clear and cold and still that it carries sound a great distance. Two people, one and a half miles from each other can converse together!

It was once stated that there are "sounds in the air of which we have no idea; and if our ears could be quickened we would hear the songs of angels, whereas we now hear only the feeble accents of our own broken prayers." What a thought!

In order for sound to be heard or made known there not only has to be air but something has to be moving the air. This movement is called by scientists, "vibration." What does the word "vibrate" mean? The definition is "to swing or move back and forth." In music, when the vibrations are regular or orderly with God's laws for music, the sound is musical or pleasant. When the vibrations are not regular or disorderly, they only make noise. An example of noise would be a glass dropping on a floor and breaking or a door slamming.

"Hear, O my people, and I will testify unto thee: O Israel...hearken unto me...I am the Lord thy God" (Psalm 81:8, 10). God had an orderly plan to accomplish the

"Hear, O my people"

announcement of Jesus' first advent to the world. Israel was to be the distinctive, vibrating instrument to do this. But instead of making beautiful, pleasant sounds, they became a discordant noise and turned from God's plan! They were not **diligent** in giving God's *"certain sound."* They became *"...as sounding brass, or a tinkling cymbal"* (I Corinthians 13:1).

We will learn more about what makes musical sound in the next lesson. Remember, that noise occurs when the vibrations are disorderly, and correct musical sound is made when the vibrations are distinct and orderly.

Reinforce

Take a piano, harp, or some other stringed instrument,* press the keys or pluck the different sizes of strings. You will see them vibrate. This is what is making the sound. Even when you put your hand down on the table, the table vibrates. Sometimes you can feel vibration and not hear it.

*If you do not have a stringed instrument available to you, find different sizes of rubber bands and string them between two nails in a piece of wood.

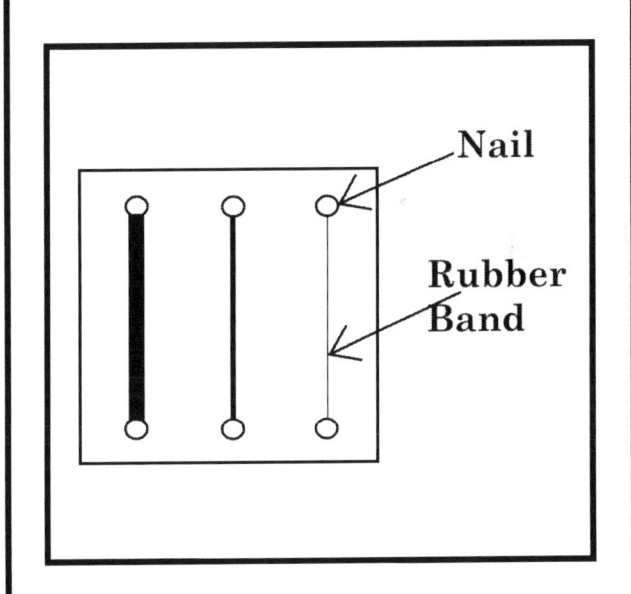

Remind

Have you heard vibrations that make noise? Usually, things that make noise are destructive; like the sound of balloons popping; a person playing loud rock music in a car beside your family car when driving down the road so that it vibrates the car you are in—this is an uncertain sound.

What Makes Sound? – Student – Page 3

Reflect
Distinct Sounds

"Ministers and teachers should discipline themselves to clear and <u>distinct</u> articulation, giving the <u>full sound</u> to every word."

Christian Education 241

"The third angel's message is to be <u>sounded</u> in clear, <u>distinct</u> language. The trumpet is to give a <u>certain sound</u>."

21 Manuscript Releases 283

"God has placed in our hands a banner upon which is inscribed, *'Here is the patience of the saints: here are they that keep the commandments of God, and the faith of Jesus'* (Revelation 14:12). This is a <u>distinct</u>, separating message—a message that is to give no <u>uncertain sound</u>."

Counsels to Writers 11

Upon rocky Patmos, Christ came to John and "addressed [him] in tones <u>distinct</u> and clear.... The tones of His [Jesus'] voice are like the <u>musical sound</u> of many waters."

Review and Herald 3-1-1881

"Those who talk rapidly, from the throat, jumbling the words together, and raising their voices to an unnaturally high pitch, soon become hoarse, and the words spoken lose half the force which they would have if spoken slowly, <u>distinctly</u>, and not so loud."

Christian Education 241

"Had all God's ministers, as faithful stewards of the grace of God, called upon the world to hear the last note of warning, giving the trumpet a <u>certain sound</u>, thousands more might have been converted, and added their voices in proclaiming the message to the world. In <u>distinct</u> notes of solemn warning is to be given the closing message that will prepare a people to receive the seal of the living God."

Bible Training School 1-1-1908

What Makes Sound? – Student – Page 4

Reinforce
A Distinct Sound

Color these letters, then read the verse.

"I WILL SING OF THE MERCIES OF THE LORD FOR EVER: WITH MY MOUTH WILL I MAKE KNOWN THY FAITHFULNESS TO ALL GENERATIONS."

PSALM 89:1

Learning How to Be Diligent

"And whatsoever ye do, do it heartily, as to the Lord, and not unto men."
Colossians 3:23

In nature, what creatures remind us of **diligence**? You might be reminded of the beaver for Job 12:7 tells us, *"But ask now the beasts, and they shall teach thee."* Or you may remember Proverbs 6:6, *"Go to the ant, thou sluggard; consider her ways, and be wise."*

How the beaver teaches us <u>diligence</u>:

Have you ever heard a person who is a hard-worker being called an "eager beaver" or that they are "busy as a beaver"? The reason for this is because beavers seem to be busy working almost all the time. They are well known for their skill as tree cutters. When a beaver cuts a tree down, it uses those strong front teeth to peel off the bark and the branches. **Diligently** the beaver works **diligently** until the tree falls to the ground. Then it begins to carry the branches into the water. These are stored deep in the water for use as food during the winter. Are you a **diligent** "eager beaver?"

How the ant teaches us <u>diligence</u>:

In the balance of nature, ants play an important role. A large number of insects are eaten by them. This helps to keep insect population down. For example, in the tropics ants eat more than half of the termites which hatch each year. Just think what would happen if ants were not **diligent** in their work! There would be more insects then we could handle. What happens when you are not **diligent** in doing your work?

Giving all I have, physically, mentally, and spiritually to complete a task assigned to me.

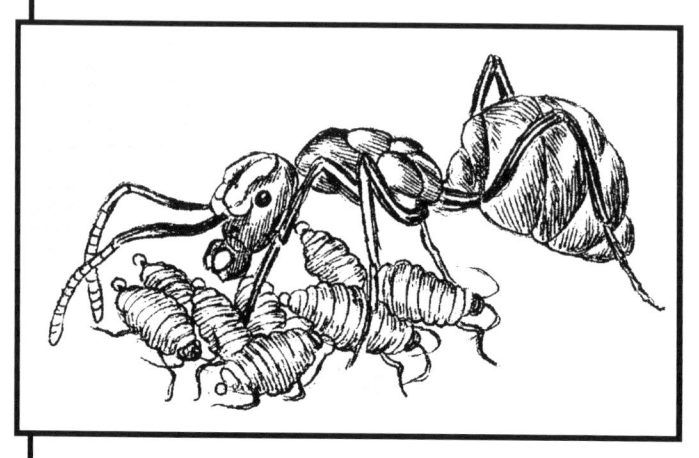

What Makes Sound? – Student – Page 6

Reinforce

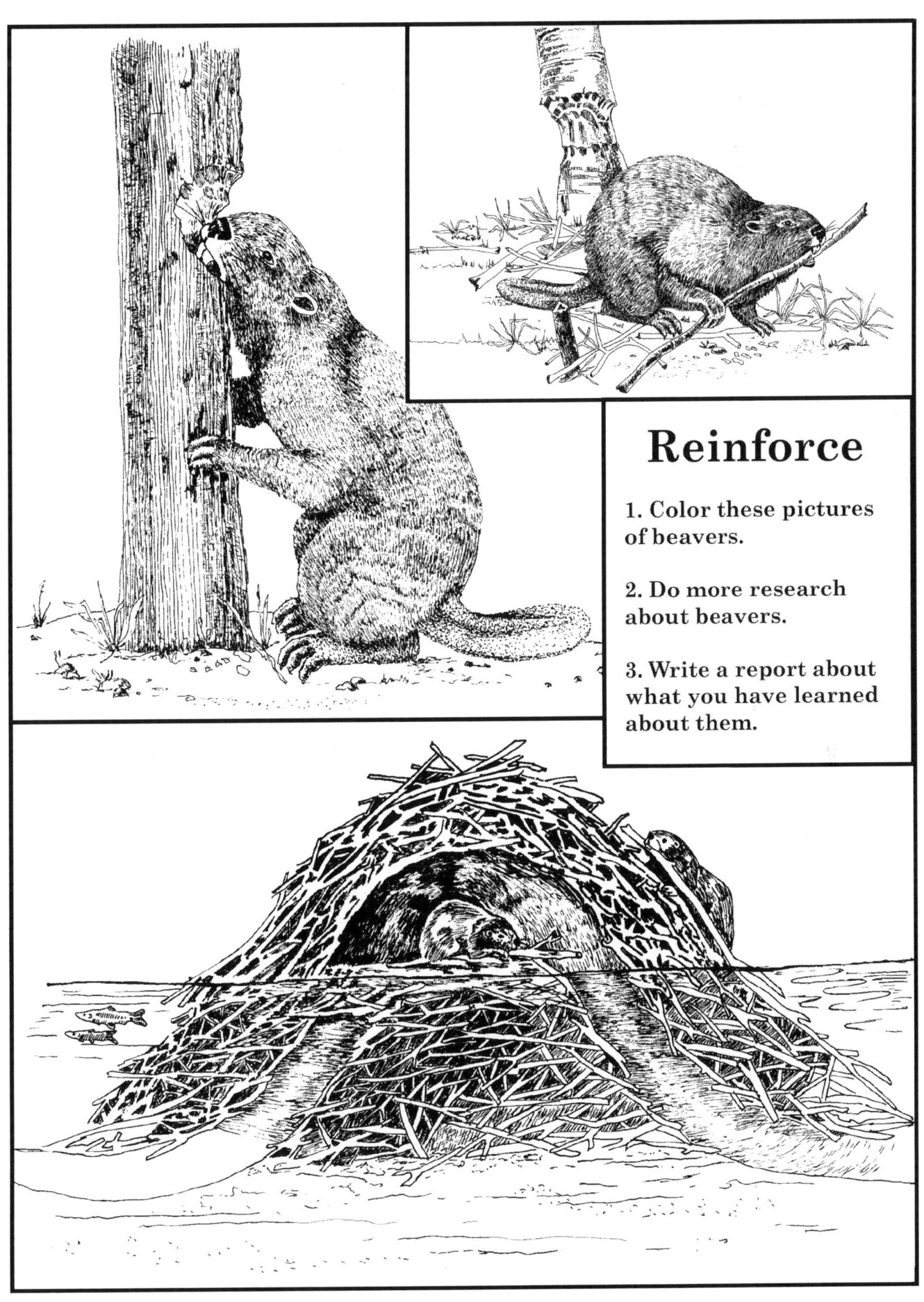

1. Color these pictures of beavers.

2. Do more research about beavers.

3. Write a report about what you have learned about them.

What Makes Sound? – Student – Page 7

What does it mean to <u>diligently</u> give a certain sound?

How I can learn <u>diligence</u> from nature:	How does this relate to "giving a certain sound" in music?
1. With God's help I will finish projects.	1. With God's help I will learn all I can about music and that "certain sound."
2. With God's help I will do the project correctly.	2. With God's help I will learn the rules and laws God has for music.
3. With God's help I will follow instructions.	3. With God's help I will follow these laws of music.
4. With God's help I will keep my mind on what I am doing.	4. With God's help I will concentrate on good music.

That is what it means to be **diligent**.

"Whatsoever ye do, do it heartily, as to the Lord, and not unto men."

Colossians 3:23

Reflect

"No man e'er was glorious who was not laborious."
—Benjamin Franklin

Oboe

What Makes Sound? – Student – Page 8

Diligence
Statements and Answers

1. I do not understand God's laws for music.

I have the Bible and my parents to guide me in this.

2. It is so complicated and takes so much time to learn.

My time and my mind belong to God—He can teach me and give me a desire to learn.

3. I have already tried.

I can learn more from each "try."

4. I just can not learn it!

Challenges will build <u>diligence</u> in my character!

> "The superior man makes the difficult to be overcome his first interest. Success comes only later."
> —Confucius

More Diligence

More **diligence** give me;
   Swift flieth the day,
Each moment some lost one
   Is passing away.

How can I be idle,
   Christ knowing so well?
More **diligence** give me,
   Love's story to tell.
   —F. E. Belden

Read a book about Thomas Edison.

Reflect

Diligence is the opposite of slothfulness.
"**Diligence** overcomes great difficulties. Sloth makes them."
   —Benjamin Franklin

What Makes Sound? – Student – Page 9

Reinforce
Place I

Help this boy and his sister find God's Laws of Music.
Be <u>diligent</u> and careful so that they do not get lost
in Satan's counterfeit music!

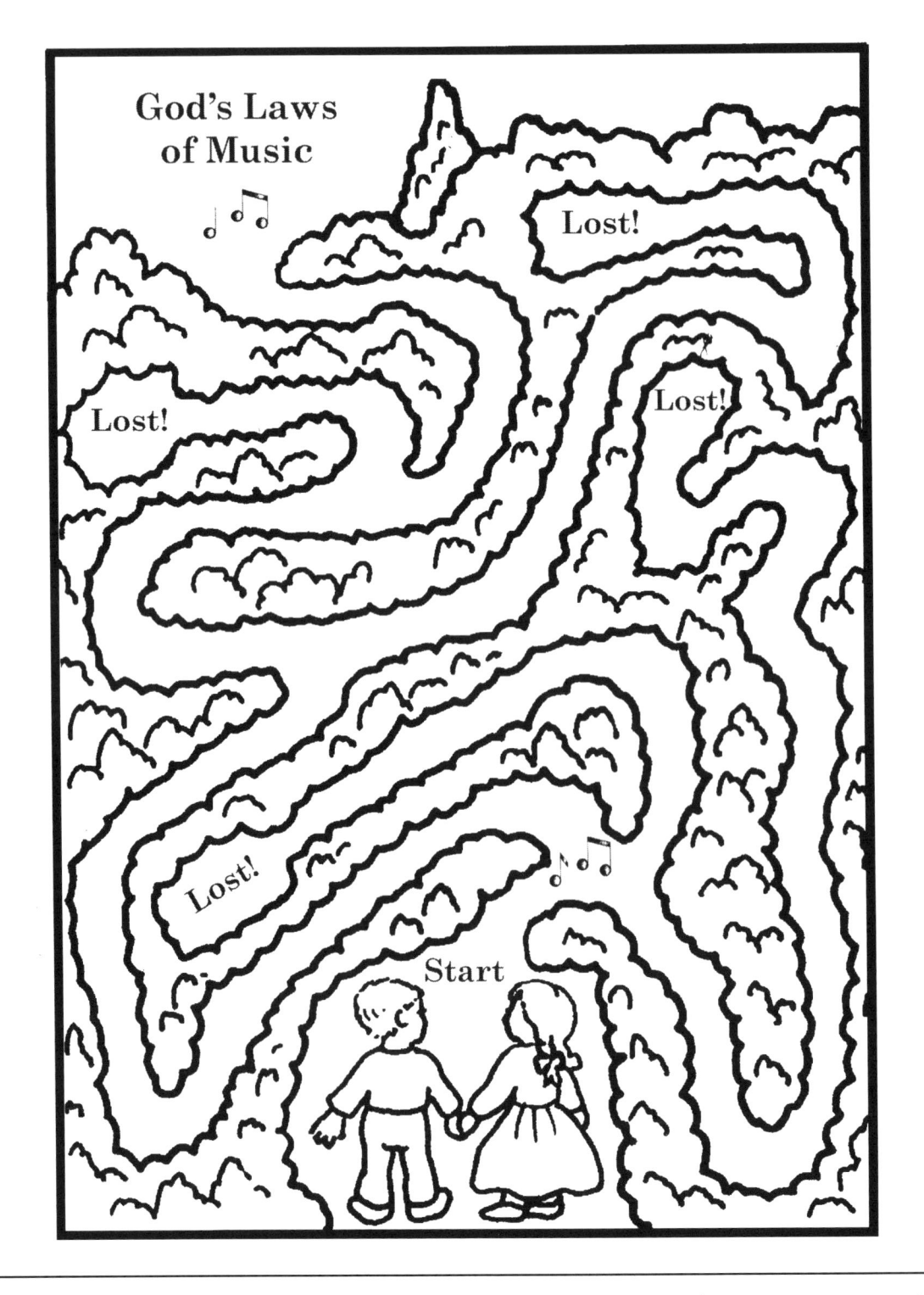

What Makes Sound? – Student – Page 10

Distinct Sounds through the Centuries

**"Give thanks unto the Lord,
<u>call</u> [sound] upon his name,
<u>make known</u> [sound] his deeds among the people."**
I Chronicles 16:8

"For more than a thousand years the Jewish people had awaited the Saviour's coming. Upon this event they had rested their brightest hopes. In <u>song</u> and <u>prophecy</u>, in <u>temple rite</u> and <u>household prayer</u>, they had enshrined His name. And yet at His coming they knew Him not. The Beloved of heaven was to them *'as a root out of a dry ground;'* and they saw in Him no beauty that they should desire Him. *'He came unto His own, and His own received Him not'* (Isaiah 53:2; John 1:11).

"Yet God had chosen Israel. He had <u>called</u> them to preserve among men the knowledge of His law, and of the symbols and prophecies that pointed to the Saviour. He desired them to be as wells of salvation to the world. What Abraham was in the land of his sojourn, what Joseph was in Egypt, and Daniel in the courts of Babylon, the Hebrew people were to be among the nations. <u>They were to reveal God to men</u>" in their <u>song</u> and <u>prophecy</u>, in <u>temple rite</u> and <u>household prayer</u>.*
They were to *"<u>make known</u> his deeds among the people"* (I Chronicles 16:8). *"And these words, which I command thee this day, shall be in thine heart: And thou shalt teach them diligently unto thy children, and shalt talk of them when thou sittest in thine house, and when thou walkest by the way, and when thou liest down, and when thou risest up"* (Deuteronomy 6:6-7).

Through the centuries, Jesus had **diligently** <u>sounded</u> a call to Israel saying, *"...I will put my law in their inward parts, and write it in their hearts; and will be their God, and they shall be my people"* (Jeremiah 31:33). *"For thou art an holy people unto the Lord thy God, and the Lord hath chosen thee to be*

*Desire of Ages 27

**"Whoso keepeth
the vine
shall eat
the fruit thereof."
—A Proverb**

What Makes Sound? – Student – Page 11

a peculiar people unto himself, above all the nations that are upon the earth" (Deuteronomy 14:2).

Jesus *"came unto his own, and his own received him not."* Why? Because they misunderstood the prophecy and expected a king and not a humble baby. He must have been very disappointed (John 1:11). Be reminded of this the next time you call brother or sister and they do not respond to you. Do not react with unkindness, but rather remember that even though Jesus was ignored it was written of Him, *"...he is kind unto the unthankful and to the evil"* (Luke 6:35). Make sure that you are **diligently** responding when your heavenly Father calls you!

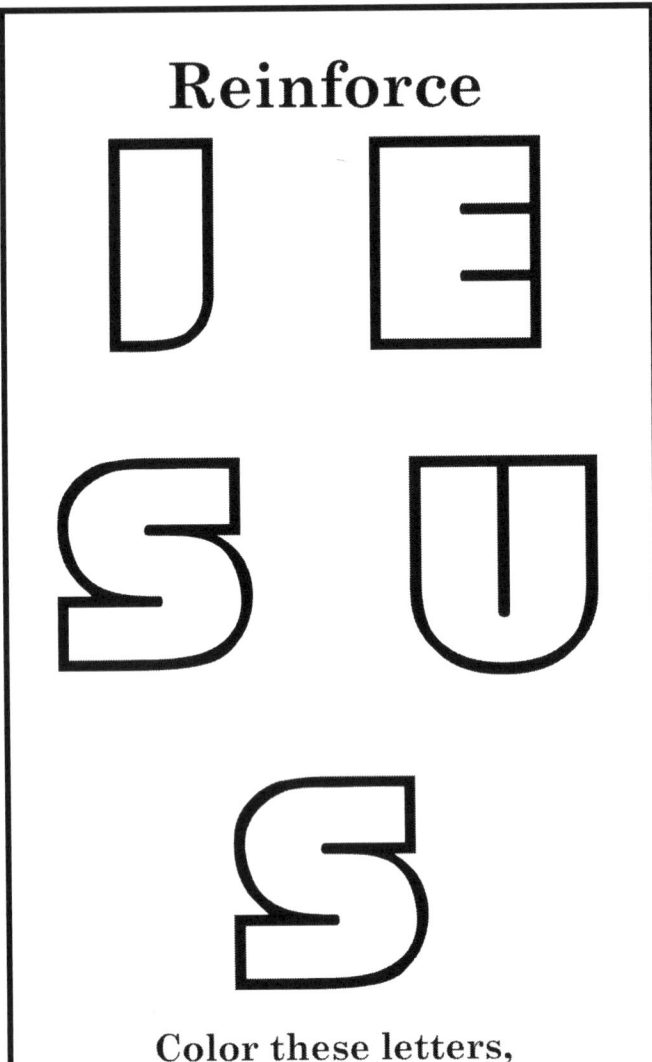

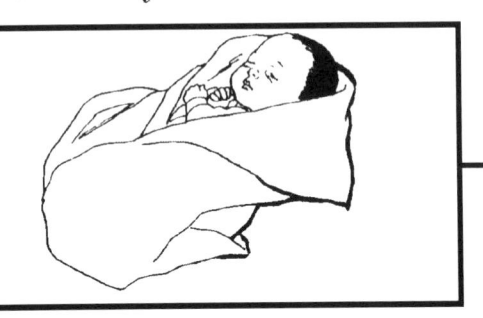

Reinforce

JESUS

Color these letters, then draw notes around them.

Remind

1. When father or mother call you to do a chore such as cleaning the kitchen or fixing lunch, <u>listen</u> carefully to all the instructions and do your chores **diligently**.

2. *"Make a joyful noise unto the Lord"* during family worship (Psalm 100:1). God delights in the <u>sound</u> of sincere praise. *"It came to pass as the trumpeters and singers were as one, to make one <u>sound</u> to be heard in praising and thanking the Lord; and when they lifted up their voice with the trumpets and cymbals and instruments of musick, and praised the Lord, saying, For he is good; for his mercy endureth for ever: that then the house was filled with a cloud, even the house of the Lord"* (II Chronicles 5:13).

What Makes Sound? – Student – Page 12

Reflect
A Certain Sound through the Centuries

Here are some ways God sent messages to His people through time. It was to help them understand the important events about to take place.

Song

Temple Rite

Prophecy

Household Prayer

Jesus Is Coming Again Very Soon!

We sing and play: "Lift up the Trumpet."

We read.

We go to church.

We study and pray.

Do we understand the messages God sends to us today? Read Revelation 14.

What Makes Sound? – Student – Page 13

Sympathetic Vibration
"...The Lord's hand is not shortened, that it cannot save; neither his ear heavy, that it cannot hear."
Isaiah 59:1

Waves of sound travel through the air. Sound waves can be affected by what may be called <u>sympathetic vibrations</u>. If two strings of an instrument are stretched out side by side and tuned to the same pitch, when one is sounded, the other will also sound. If a person sounds one of the strings, and then with his hand, stops its vibrations, the sound of the other string next to it can be heard.

God had chosen Israel. He wanted to use them to produce a sympathetic vibration that would resound from the ends of the earth. But they did not respond to His touch. They had become <u>too slack</u> in their obedience to God. Like a <u>loose string</u> on an instrument, they could not respond to even the Master's divine touch. It is written, "Behold, *the Lord's hand is not shortened, that it cannot save; neither his ear heavy, that it cannot hear: But your iniquities have separated between you and your God, and your sins have hid his face from you, that he will not hear*" (Isaiah 59:1-2).

Reflect

"Wherefore, when I came, was there no man? when I called, was there none to answer? Is my hand shortened at all, that it cannot redeem? or have I no power to deliver?..."
Isaiah 50:2

"Is any thing too hard for the Lord?..."
Genesis 18:14

"...Is the Lord's hand waxed short? thou shalt see now whether my word shall come to pass unto thee or not."
Numbers 11:23

"Ah Lord God! behold, thou hast made the heaven and the earth by thy great power and stretched out arm, and there is nothing too hard for thee."
Jeremiah 32:17

Reflect
Vibrations

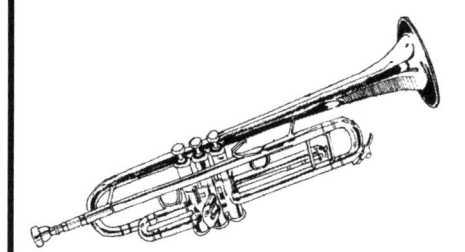

"Not a sigh is breathed,
not a pain felt,
not a grief
pierces the soul,
but the throb
<u>vibrates</u>
to the
Father's heart."

The Desire of Ages 356

"Those who have
acted the most
prominent part
in the rejection
and crucifixion
of Christ
come forth
to see Him
as He is
[at the second
advent]...
The voice
which
they heard
so often
in entreaty
and persuasion
will again
<u>sound</u>
in their ears.
Every tone
of gracious
solicitation
will <u>vibrate</u>
as distinctly
in their ears
as when
the Saviour
spoke in
the synagogues
and on
the street."

*Last Day
Events* 275

"It is God's plan that every part
of His government shall depend
on every other part,
the whole as a wheel
within a wheel,
working with entire harmony.
He moves upon human forces,
causing His Spirit to touch
invisible chords,
and the <u>vibration</u>
rings to the extremity
of the universe."

Evangelism 93

"Your influence
reaches the soul;
you touch
not a wire
but that
<u>vibrates</u>
back to God."

My Life Today 178

"The humblest workers,
in co-operation with Christ,
may touch chords whose <u>vibrations</u>
shall ring to the ends of the earth
and make melody
throughout eternal ages."

The Ministry of Healing 159

Clarinet

"Let it not be
that the sympathetic cords,
which should be quick to <u>vibrate</u>
at the least touch,
shall be cold as steel, frozen, as it were,
and unable to help where help is needed."

Our High Calling 184

What Makes Sound? – Student – Page 15

"We are to strike a keynote that will <u>vibrate</u> to every soul, and bring joy to the heavenly intelligences."

Review and Herald 10-16-1900

"The pleasure of doing good animates the mind, and <u>vibrates</u> through the whole body."

Christian Temperance 102

"The pure in heart see God in every providence, in every phase of true education. They <u>vibrate</u> to the first approach of light which radiates from the throne of God."

Fundamentals of Christian Education 414

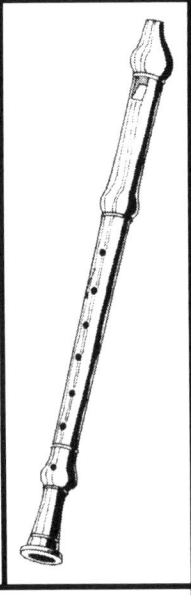

"Should not our souls be in that condition that every chord of the harp of our being shall <u>vibrate</u> with praises to God when touched by the finger of His love!"

2 Sermons and Talks 50

Remind

Keep your soul in a state of sympathetic vibration with heaven by **diligently** studying and then putting into practice what you have learned. God wants you to be like a harp swept by heavenly breezes.

Reinforce

1. If you have access to a tuning fork, sound it and then hold it until it is no longer heard. Then set it upon a board and notice that the sound will be so reinforced by the sympathetic vibrations that it will once more be heard.

2. Touch the key of a piano in such a way as to raise the hammer from the string without producing sound. Now, give the same note by your voice or another instrument, and then stop. The string will be heard to sound in sympathetic vibration.

What Makes Sound? – Student – Page 16

The Symphony Orchestra

Woodwinds

Strings

Conductor

Brass

Percussion

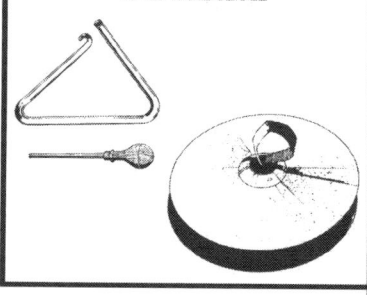

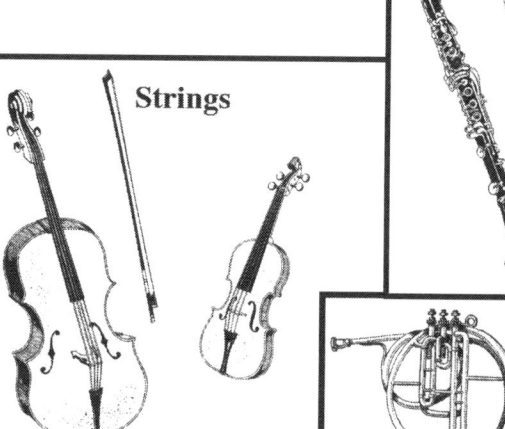

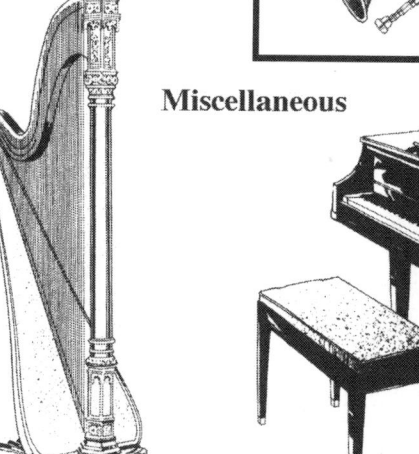

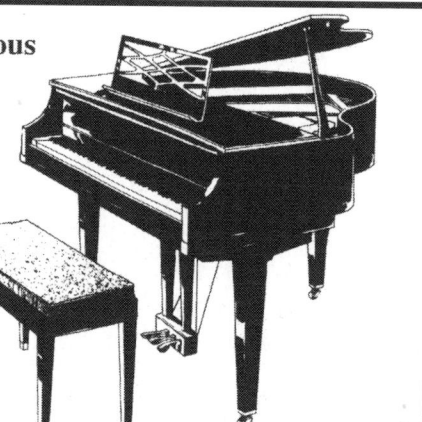

Miscellaneous

"**Make a joyful noise unto the Lord, all ye lands.**"
Psalm 100:1

Research
How Wind Instruments Make Sound

"Blessed are they that...seek him with the whole heart."
Psalm 119:2

Sound is produced in a wind instrument by blowing into or through a tube. Vibrations are confined to the column of air they occupy. The size of the column determines the pitch of the sound just as the size of a string on a stringed instrument determines its pitch. This reminds us how we can limit God's ability to use us as instruments for His work. He needs us to be <u>completely</u> consecrated to Him so we can <u>make Him known</u> to this perishing world. It is written, *"Blessed are they that...seek him with the <u>whole</u> heart"* (Psalm 119:2). "Men are instruments in the hand of God, employed by Him to accomplish His purposes of grace and mercy. Each has his part to act; to each is granted a measure of light, adapted to the necessities of his time, and sufficient to enable him to perform the work which God has given him to do."*

The deeper our relationship with God, the deeper we will search for His truth and His will for our lives, and the higher we will soar like eagles. *"And ye shall seek me and find me, when ye shall search for me with <u>all</u> our heart"* (Jeremiah 29:13). *"Then shalt thou delight thyself in the Lord; and I will cause thee to ride upon the high places of the earth..."* (Isaiah 58:14). As we dedicate our music, both vocal and instrumental, to God so must we be consecrated instruments to Him. Then we shall stand up for Jesus and **diligently** sound the praise of God!

"And many strokes, though with a little axe, hewn down and fell the hardest-timbered oak."

—William Shakespeare

Reinforce

Will sound travel through liquid?

Items needed:
1. A container filled with water
2. Two rocks

What you do:
Take the two rocks and hold them down in the water. Next strike them together forcibly. Did you hear a sound?

---

*Great Controversy 343

What Makes Sound? – Student – Page 17

Stand Up, Stand Up For Jesus

The story behind the words.

What does it take to inspire the writing of a hymn? In the case of "Stand Up, Stand Up For Jesus," it took the dying words of a clergyman. The young clergyman was Dudley Atkins Tyng and the minister who wrote the poem was George Duffeld, Jr.

Tyng was bold, fearless, and uncompromising as a preacher. Although young, success attended him and his congregation grew. In addition to his duties as a pastor, Tyng began noonday lectures at the Y.M.C.A. His fame grew and so did the crowds which came to hear his sermons and addresses.

On a Tuesday in March 1858 there were over 5,000 men gathered for a huge meeting sponsored by the Y.M.C.A. Tyng's sermon, "Ye that are men, go and serve the Lord," was from Exodus 10:11. Many received the message and the entire city was being aroused.

During the sermon Pastor Tyng stated, "I must tell my Master's errand, and I would rather that this right arm were amputated at the trunk than that I should come short of my duty to you in delivering God's message."

The following week this minister returned to his family in the country. Upon his return, he was in his barn witnessing the operation of a corn-thrasher. The date was Tuesday, April 13, 1858. As a mule was walking up the inclined plane of the machine, Tyng raised his arm to place his hand on the mule's head. But suddenly his morning gown's loose sleeve caught between the cogs! The arm became lacerated severely and the main artery severed with the median nerve injured. Only four days later mortification had set in and his right arm was amputated very close to the shoulder. Anxiety prevailed for his life. Yet the shock to his system proved fatal two days later.

A newspaper reporter gave a detailed account of Tyng's passing. One thing he wrote was this, "Taking his [Tyng's] aged father's hand, he said with much earnestness, 'Stand up for Jesus, father; stand up for Jesus; and tell my

What Makes Sound? – Student – Page 18

brethren of the ministry, wherever you meet them, to stand up for Jesus.'" Thus, this faithful soul, surrounded by his family, and his intellect unclouded, died.

At the memorial service Pastor George Duffield, Jr. heard the account of his friend's passing. He said, "Tyng was one of the noblest, bravest, and manliest men I have ever met." Not too long after this he preached a sermon from Ephesians 6:14, *"Stand, therefore, having your loins girt about with truth...."* Concluding his sermon he read an original poem of six stanzas. Duffield explained that this poem had been inspired by his co-worker's dying words.

Are you standing up for Jesus? Are you giving that certain sound?

Stand Up For Jesus

Stand up! stand up for Jesus!
Ye soldiers of the cross;
Lift high His royal banner,
It must not suffer loss:
From vict'ry unto vict'ry,
His army shall He lead,
Till ev'ry foe is vanquished,
And Christ is Lord indeed.

Stand up! stand up for Jesus!
The trumpet call obey;
Forth to the mighty conflict,
In this His glorious day:
Ye that are His now serve Him,
Against unnumbered foes;
Let courage rise with danger,
And strength to strength oppose.

Stand up! stand up for Jesus!
Stand in His strength alone;
The arm of flesh will fail you;
Ye dare not trust your own:
Put on the gospel armor,
And, watching unto pray'r,
Where duty calls, or danger,
Be never wanting there.

Stand up! stand up for Jesus!
The strife will not be long;
This day the noise of battle,
The next the victor's song:
To him that overcometh,
A crown of life shall be;
He with the King of Glory
Shall reign eternally.
—*St. Gall's*

Two Types of Wind Instruments
"...And the people piped with pipes, and rejoiced with great joy, so that the earth rent with the sound of them"
I Kings 1:40

(1) Woodwinds

Woodwinds at one time were all made of wood, but today they are also made of metal or other materials. Some wind instruments are played by blowing through a mouthpiece into the instrument. A recorder is an example of this type of woodwind. Some others are played by blowing air across a hole in the instrument, such as flutes and piccolos. Others are played by blowing into a mouthpiece with one or two reeds attached to it. A reed is a thin, flexible piece of cane, plastic, or metal fastened to the mouthpiece or over an air opening in a musical instrument. The reed is set in vibration as the air from the musician's breath passes over it. When the Holy Spirit passes over us we begin to "vibrate" for God.

The pitch is controlled by placing the fingers on holes or keys that cover the holes. This makes the column of air shorter or longer, depending on which holes are open or closed. The piccolo and flute have the highest pitches, while the bassoon and the contra bassoon have the lowest. The shorter and/or smaller the column of air, the higher the pitch; the longer and/or larger the column of air, the lower the pitch. There is a lesson in this for us. Small duties, like sweeping the floor, done **diligently** are esteemed highly by the Saviour. *"He that is faithful in that which is least is faithful also in much..."* (Luke 16:10). How **diligent** are you in doing the small duties in your home?

Piccolo

Remarkable Fact

"Wood is a good conductor of sound. [Many years ago] In Sweden, deaf men and women may be seen sitting in church holding in their mouths long wooden sticks which touch the pulpit. By doing this they are enabled to hear much of the sermon."
—*Eliza H. Morton*

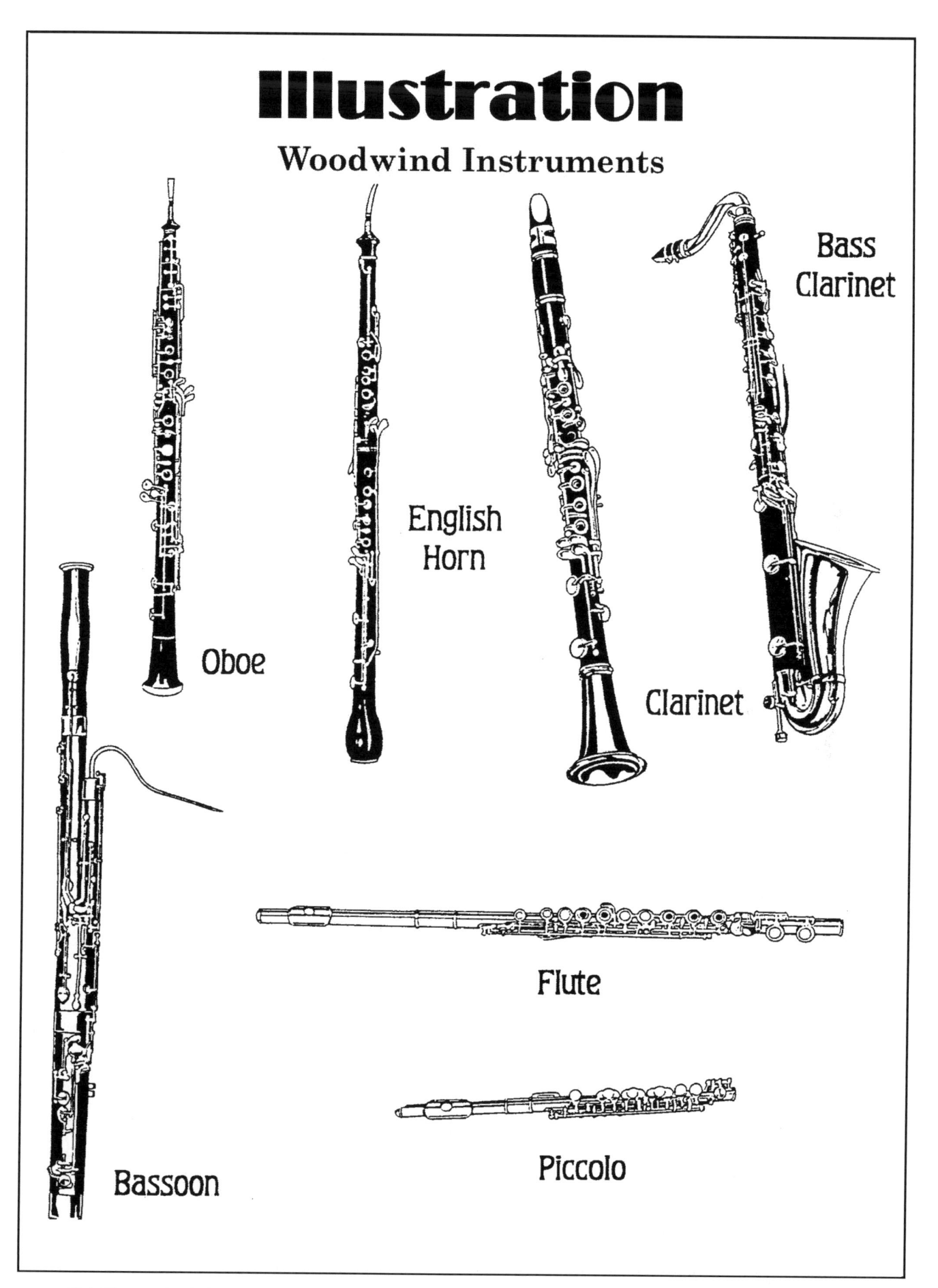

Illustration
Woodwind Instruments

Oboe

English Horn

Clarinet

Bass Clarinet

Bassoon

Flute

Piccolo

(2) Brass

Brass instruments are played by placing the lips on the instrument so that when blowing into it the lips vibrate. The lips are made to vibrate like reeds by tensing or relaxing them, which produces different pitches. The tighter the lips the higher the pitch, the looser the lips the lower the pitch.

The player can further control the pitch by valves which shorten or lengthen the tube into which the air is blown.

The major instruments of brass in an orchestra are the French horn, trumpet, trombone, and tuba. Some brass instruments have slides instead of valves.

It requires deep breathing to play brass wind instruments. Who is it that gives us breath? It is written, *"And the Lord God formed man of the dust of the ground, and breathed into his nostrils the breath of life..." "The spirit of God hath made me, and the breath of the Almighty hath given me life"* (Genesis 2:7; Job 33:4). God supplies our breath. We use that breath to make sound.

God vibrates us to **diligently** give a certain sound for Him! Are you willing to do your part in sounding out the distinctive message for this time in earth's history? *"Even things without life giving sound, whether pipe or harp, except they give a distinction in the sounds, how shall it be known what is piped or harped? For if the trumpet give an uncertain sound, who shall prepare himself to the battle?"* (I Corinthians 14:7-8).

Reinforce
A Certain Sound

1. Read Numbers 10:2-10.

2. Notice people's necks. Do you think there is a relationship between the width and length of a person's neck (throat) and the pitch of their voice? Compare the voice of children to that of grown-up people.

3. Read the story, "Little Performances."

What Makes Sound? – Student – Page 22

Illustration

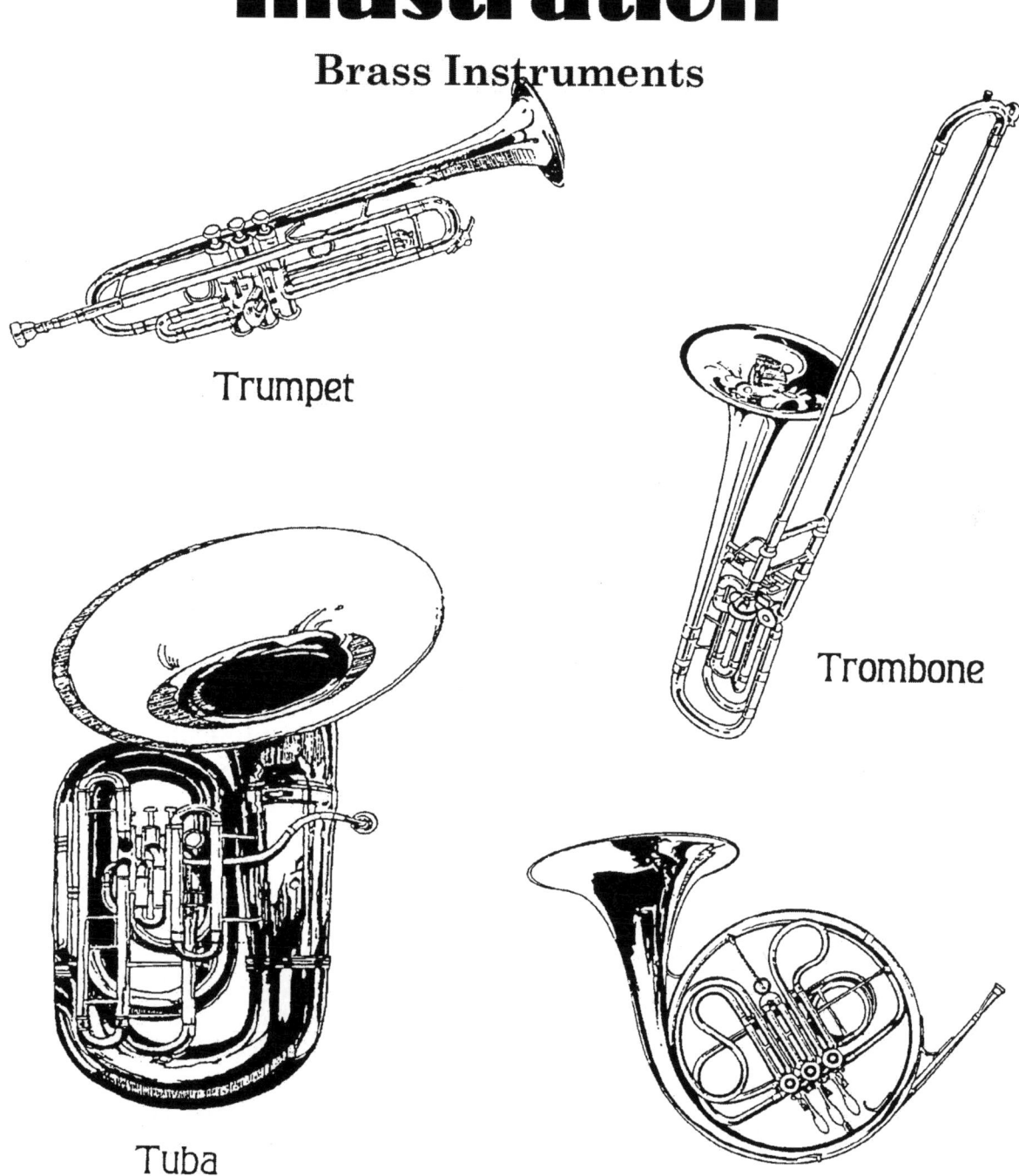

Brass Instruments

Trumpet

Trombone

Tuba

French Horn

"Blow ye the trumpet in Zion, and sound an alarm
in my holy mountain: let all the inhabitants
of the land tremble: for the day of the Lord cometh,
for it is nigh at hand."
Joel 2:1

What Makes Sound? – Student – Page 23

Little Performances

"The only thing that marred the trip through Norway," recounted a newly returned traveler, "was a little girl in the party who annoyed us all by persisting in drumming on the piano in every hotel at which we stopped. She could play only one tiresome little tune, and that with one finger. In every hotel, she would run into the parlor, and forthwith our ears would be assailed with that wearisome tune. It annoyed us all so much that we were thinking of appealing to her mother to stop it.

"One day we drove up to a strange hotel. As usual, the child made for the parlor and begun to play her simple and monotonous little tune. A great musician was stopping at the hotel. He came to the threshold of the parlor, listened a moment, and then went over to the little girl at the piano. He put his hands over hers, and using the tedious little melody as a theme, he began to improvise. As he played, the beauty of the harmony and the curiously attractive rhythm he gave to the music caught the ears of every one who was within hearing. The room became filled with breathless listeners, who, when he finished, began to applaud. The musician rose, smiled, and taking the little girl's hands, said, 'It is your music they applaud.'"

So it is with our best efforts that seem to produce so little of the effect we desire. Some day we shall see that our Heavenly Father has been joining His power to ours to produce results more marvelous than any we had dreamed of. Our tiresome little performances He will transform into glorious symphonies. Whoever works faithfully for God at life's humdrum tasks works not alone. Over his hands the unseen hands of God are placed. The results are divine, but God calls them ours.

> "The falling drop at last will wear the stone."
> —Lucretius

Review
Place I - II - III

1. Sound means:

   _ _   _ _ _ _ _ _ _ _

2. What are some ways that sound is produced?

3. Can there be sound without air?

4. What does it mean to be **diligent**?

5. What is the definition of "vibrate?"

6. What does it mean to give a certain sound? What about an uncertain sound?

7. Define the word distinct.

8. What is the difference between noise and pure musical sound?

9. When Jesus came to this world, how many years had the Jewish people been waiting for Him? What four ways had they enshrined His name?

10. What did God want His chosen people to **diligently** do for Him on earth? Why did they not see beauty in Jesus?

11. What is sympathetic vibration?

12. On the following lines write the word **higher** or **lower,** after each condition for wind instruments, according to the pitch each will have:

(A) Shorter column of air _____

(B) A longer column of air _____

(C) Tightened lips for a brass instrument_____

(D) Loosened lips for a brass instrument _____

(E) A very wide column of air _____

(F) A very narrow column of air ___

13. What are two cases in the Bible of God calling someone? To where were they called?

14. What is God calling you to do?

Reinforce

1. Go to a music store (or use an encyclopedia or other resource books if you are not near a music store) **and observe wind instruments. Diligently** try to see the different sizes of air columns, valves, slides, keys, and holes. Also, notice their overall size. Take a note pad and write down different facts about each one. Do they have valves, what kind of mouthpiece do they have, do they have large (wide) columns of air or narrow columns, short or long, etc.? Discuss, as a family, each instrument you saw using the facts you learned in the lesson. Where do the wind instruments fit in the orchestra? (See Lesson 1.)

2. Make a Bull-Roarer Musical Instrument.

Items needed:
1. 4–6 inch long cardboard tube. The kind of cardboard paper towels are wound on will do.
2. Flat clothing elastic band, 1/4 inch wide and 20 inches long.
3. String.

What you do:
Thread the elastic through the tube. Tie a knot in it. Take the string and tie it onto the elastic (as shown in picture). Now you have a bull-roarer musical instrument. To make it work, swing it above your head faster and still faster. It should make a loud humming sound. This instrument only works when wind rushes through it.

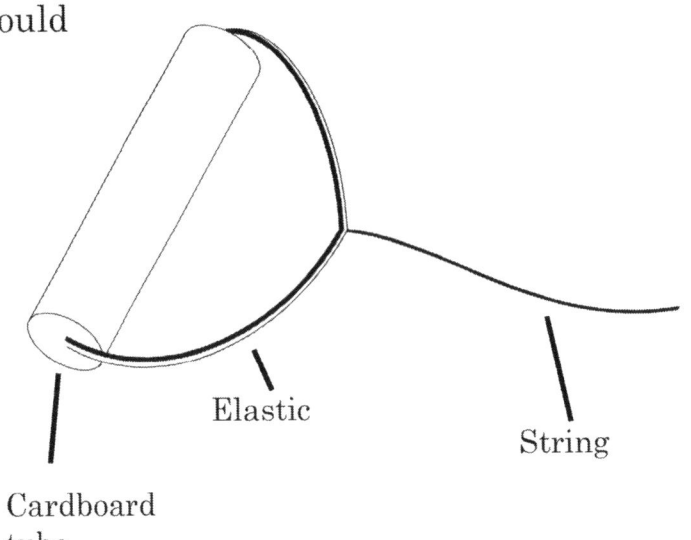

What Makes Sound? – Student – Page 26

Remainder
An Uncertain Sound

"Come, and let us return unto the Lord: for he hath torn, and he will heal us; he hath smitten, and he will bind us up."
Hosea 6:1

"As they departed from God, the Jews in a great degree lost sight of the teaching of the ritual service. That service had been instituted by Christ Himself. In every part it was a symbol of Him; and it had been full of vitality and spiritual beauty. But the Jews lost the spiritual life from their ceremonies, and clung to the dead forms. They trusted to the sacrifices and ordinances themselves, instead of resting upon Him to whom they pointed. In order to supply the place of that which they had lost, the priests and rabbis multiplied requirements of their own; and the more rigid they grew, the less of the love of God was manifested. They measured their holiness by the multitude of their ceremonies, while their hearts were filled with pride and hypocrisy."*

The Israelites became a uncertain, disorderly noise as they departed from God. The only way to be a distinct, pleasant sound and <u>make known</u> Jesus' Second Coming is to **diligently** draw close to God. And the promise is if we *"Draw nigh to God...he will draw nigh to you"* (James 4:8).

Reflect

"The block of granite, which was an obstacle in the path of the weak, becomes a stepping stone in the path of the strong."
—*Thomas Carlyle*

Let us not repeat the mistake of the Jews.
"They profess [uncertain sound] *that they know God; but in works they deny him, being...disobedient, and unto every good work reprobate."*
Titus 1:16

*Desire of Ages 29

What Makes Sound? – Student – Page 27

Mark Your Bible

Sounds

What are some things that make sounds?

1. Leaves

Leviticus 26:36 – "...The sound of a shaken leaf...."

2. The sky

Psalm 77:17 – "The clouds poured out water: the skies sent out a sound...."

3. Rain

I Kings 18:41 – "...There is a sound of abundance of rain."

4. A battle

Jeremiah 50:22 – "A sound of battle is in the land, and of great destruction."

5. Musical instruments

Job 21:12 – "They take the timbrel and harp, and rejoice at the sound of the organ."

I Chronicles 16:42 – "...Make a sound, with the musical instruments of God."

6. Singing

I Chronicles 15:19 – "So the singers...were appointed to sound with cymbals of brass."

7. Wings of the cherubims

Ezekiel 10:5 – "And the sound of the cherubims' wings was heard...."

8. The voice of God

Revelation 1:15 – "...His voice as the sound of many waters."

What are a few different qualities of sounds?

1. Loud

Psalm 150:5 – "Praise him upon the loud cymbals...."

Exodus 19:19 – "And when the voice of the trumpet sounded long; and waxed louder and louder; Moses spake, and God answered him by a voice."

What Makes Sound? – Student – Page 28

I Kings 1:40 – *"And all the people came up after him, and the people piped with pipes, and rejoiced with great joy, so that the earth rent with the sound of them."*

Matthew 24:31 – *"And he [God] shall send his angels with a great sound of a trumpet, and they shall gather together his elect from the four winds, from one end of heaven to the other."*

2. High pitch

Psalm 150:5 – *"Praise him upon the...high sounding cymbals."*

3. Long

Exodus 19:19 – *"...The voice of the trumpet sounded long...."*

4. Solemn

Psalm 92:3 – *"Upon an instrument of ten strings, and upon the psaltery; upon the harp with a solemn sound."*

5. Dreadful

Job 15:21 – *"A dreadful sound is in his ears...."*

6. Joyful

Psalm 89:15 – *"Blessed is the people that know the joyful sound: they shall walk, O Lord, in the light of thy countenance."*

Psalm 98:6 – *"With trumpets and sound of cornet make a joyful noise before the Lord, the King."*

(See also I Chronicles 15:16.)

Sound had a special use in the sanctuary service.

Exodus 28:34-35 – *"A golden bell and a pomegranate, upon the hem of the robe round about.*

"And it shall be upon Aaron to minister: and his sound shall be heard when he goeth in unto the holy place before the Lord, and when he cometh before the Lord, and when he cometh out, that he die not."

There were bells on the high priest's robe. When he went into the holy place of the sanctuary these bells would sound. This <u>made known</u> to the people that he was yet alive.

Sound has a special use today.

Psalm 150:3 – *"Praise him with the sound of the trumpet...."*

As we use sound to praise the Lord, it <u>makes known</u> that God still reigns.

Mark Your Bible
Wind Instruments

1. The first term in the Bible that refers to wind instruments is organ. Strong's defines this word as, "breathing; a reed-instrument of music." In the Bible Jubal was the first mentioned wind instrument maker.

Genesis 4:21 – *"...Jubal: he was the father of all such as handle the harp and <u>organ</u> [reed instrument]."*

2. Satan has used wind instruments but this does not make them bad.

Daniel 3:5 – *"...At what time ye hear the sound of the cornet, <u>flute</u>, harp, sackbut, psaltery, dulcimer, and all kinds of musick, ye fall down and worship the golden image that Nebuchadnezzar the king hath set up."*

Isaiah 5:12 – *"And the harp, and the viol, the tabret, and <u>pipe</u> [flute], and wine, are in their feasts: but they regard not the work of the Lord, neither consider the operation of his hands."*

3. Wind instruments should be used to praise the Lord.

Psalm 150:4 – *"Praise him with...stringed instruments and <u>organs</u> [reed instrument]."*

4. These are instruments of rejoicing.

Job 21:12 – *"They take the timbrel and harp, and rejoice at the sound of the <u>organ</u> [reed instrument]."*

I Kings 1:40 – *"And all the people came up after him, and the people <u>piped</u> with <u>pipes</u> [flute], and rejoiced with great joy, so that the earth rent with the sound of them."*

Isaiah 30:29 – *"Ye shall have a song, as in the night when a holy solemnity is kept; and gladness of heart, as when one goeth with a <u>pipe</u> [flute] to come into the mountain of the Lord, to the mighty One of Israel."*

Psalm 98:6 – *"With <u>trumpets</u> and sound of cornet make a joyful noise before the Lord, the King."*

What Makes Sound? – Student – Page 30

Outline of School Program

Age	Grade	Program
Birth through Age 7	Babies Kindergarten and Pre-school	*Family Bible Lessons* (This includes: Bible, Science–Nature, and Character)
Age 8	First Grade	*Family Bible Lessons* (This includes: Bible, Science–Nature, and Character) + Language Program (*Writing and Spelling Road to Reading and Thinking* [WSRRT])
Age 9-14 or 15	Second through Eighth Grade	*The Desire of all Nations* (This includes: Health, Mathematics, Music, Science–Nature, History/Geography/Prophecy, Language, and Voice–Speech) + Continue using WSRRT
Ages 15 or 16-19	Ninth through Twelfth Grade	9 – *Cross and Its Shadow I** + Appropriate Academic Books 10 – *Cross and Its Shadow II** + Appropriate Academic Books 11 – *Daniel the Prophet** + Appropriate Academic Books 12 – *The Seer of Patmos** (Revelation) + Appropriate Academic Books *or you could continue using *The Desire of Ages*
Ages 20-25	College	Apprenticeship

Printed in Great Britain
by Amazon